I0763721

Contents

The Shared Quilt

Evelyn Moore parked near the edge of the hospital lot, where the pavement thinned and the gravel began. As she stepped out of the car, the dampness of the spring air clung to her skin, a light mist falling gently, wrapping her in its embrace. The spaces nearer the entrance filled quickly, and she had learned to avoid circling when she was already tired. From here, she could walk at her own pace without feeling hurried. Each step crunched on the gravel, a sound that matched the determination in her heart. The building sat back from the road on a mild rise, wide and low, newer glass joined to older concrete, the seam between them plain to see. The early morning fog hung low, softening the line of the fir trees beyond the property. It was spring, though the morning still held a chill.

Inside, the hospital carried on without ceremony. People moved through the hallways, clipboards tucked under arms, voices low. Others sat along the walls, coats folded over laps, eyes fixed on nothing in particular. Evelyn passed the admitting desk without stopping and followed the route she knew by habit more than thought. She did not rush. She had learned that moving steadily took less out of her than trying to keep up.

The infusion room faced the service side of the building. A long strip of windows ran along the wall, looking out on the loading dock. Trucks arrived and left throughout the morning, small enough to maneuver easily, large enough to carry all that was needed. A man in a reflective vest unloaded crates one by one, stacking them neatly against the wall before returning for more. Food. Medical supplies. Linens. The work continued at an even pace, predictable and contained, something to look at without needing to think about it.

Evelyn checked in at the desk, gave her name, and took the clipboard. She chose a chair near the window, where she preferred to sit. As she settled, she noticed the room was cool, the air not warmed by the vents. People sat in these chairs for an hour, sometimes two, staying still as the medicine entered their bodies. She glanced at the blanket basket, an important fixture in the room, offering warmth and comfort as patients waited.

The nurse came over with a smile that Evelyn recognized.

"Morning," she said, already glancing at the chart. "How'd you do after last week?"

Evelyn let out a short breath. "I got through it."

"That's all we're asking," the nurse said. She swabbed Evelyn's skin, quick and practiced. "Any nausea today?"

Evelyn shook her head.

"Good. We'll keep it that way if we can." The needle, a brief sting, tape, and then the familiar settling as the line found its place. The nurse smoothed the tape down with her thumb. "You tell me if it starts burning."

As other patients came in, they reached for the basket of blankets near the wall. A man across the aisle pulled one up to his chin and closed his eyes. A woman near the television tucked hers around her shoulders and leaned back as if she had been waiting for that moment all morning. The heat vents hummed, steady and impersonal.

When the nurse returned to Evelyn, glancing at the blanket basket, she stopped and frowned.

"We're out. I'll bring more in a moment. I won't forget."

Evelyn nodded.

Next to Evelyn sat a woman she hadn't seen before, around her age. Hair pulled back. Jeans, sweater, practical shoes. Across her legs lay a quilt, heavy and unmistakably handmade, the fabric worn gently with use, the edges folded with care rather than bunched.

When the nurse stepped away, the woman glanced at Evelyn's hands placed beneath her thighs.

"You're cold," she said.

"A little," Evelyn admitted.

The woman lifted the edge of the quilt. "You want to share? It's large enough."

There was nothing careful about it, no performance of kindness. Evelyn hesitated a moment, then nodded. The woman scooted her chair closer, and together they arranged the quilt between them, smoothing it so it covered both their legs.

"I'm Claire," the woman said.

"Evelyn."

Claire touched the fabric lightly, almost absent-minded. "The volunteers at the church made this," she said. "It's my favorite."

The drip settled into its rhythm, a quiet, steady presence that let time stretch. The room stayed cool, but the quilt changed the way Evelyn noticed it. The cold no longer reached her first. She felt the fabric's thickness across her legs and the presence of another person beside her, one who did not seem to want anything from her at all.

She let her shoulders drop. She hadn't realized she had lifted them so tight.

Silence gathered between them, but it was the kind that stayed put once it arrived. It didn't press or hover. It simply existed. Evelyn noticed she was watching the loading dock without the usual vigilance. The man below lifted crate after crate, paused once to straighten, then went back to work. The repetition steadied her.

"They never get the temperature right in here," Claire said, her voice muted, almost conversational.

Evelyn gave a small nod. "The nurses come in and out too fast. I don't think they notice."

Claire smiled, not opening her eyes. "But we notice."

That was true in a way Evelyn didn't bother to test. She shifted slightly, careful not to disturb the quilt. It stayed where it was, covering both of them without needing adjustment.

They talked after that, loosely, without deciding to. Claire mentioned that her sessions were on Tuesdays since she started. Evelyn said hers were Fridays, but she changed last week. They spoke about the fog, how it sometimes burned off by noon and sometimes stayed all day. Claire said she lived close to town. Evelyn said she lived farther up the hill, closer to the hospital.

When the nurse returned with a stack of blankets tucked under one arm, she slowed, took in the scene, and smiled.

"Looks like you two solved it," she said.

Evelyn and Claire both nodded. The nurse continued without another word.

Claire finished first. The nurse disconnected her line and reminded her of next week's appointment. Claire sat for a moment after, letting herself gather. Then she stood, one hand leaning on the chair.

"Since you switched your schedule," she said, slipping her bag onto her shoulder, "I'll see you next week."

Evelyn looked up at her and smiled. "Thanks for sharing the quilt."

Claire nodded, as if that settled something, and headed for the door.

Evelyn watched her leave. An unfamiliar feeling swelled in her chest. Not relief. Not gratitude exactly. More like a surprising expansion, as if she had made room for something new, and she wasn't quite as alone as she thought she'd be.

Her own treatment stopped not long after. She waited while the nurse finished, then stood and gathered up her things. She folded the quilt carefully and placed it back, reluctant without knowing why. She passed the blanket basket, now full again, passed the long window, the dock still moving at its steady pace, and moved into the hallway.

The next week, the air seemed lighter, leaning more into the spring. Evelyn arrived at the same time and took the same chair. Claire was already there, IV in place, a book open in her lap. When they saw each other, they smiled, the recognition easy.

"Good to see you again," Claire said.

The nurse started Evelyn's line and moved on. The vents shifted, and the room warmed slightly. Claire lifted the quilt without looking up, and Evelyn leaned in as if it were already agreed upon. The fabric settled across their legs. Evelyn sensed something ease inside her, a letting go she hadn't known she'd been holding back.

"You always bring a book," Evelyn said.

Claire glanced down at it. "I like having somewhere to go in my mind while I'm here. Even if it doesn't go far."

Evelyn nodded. "I used to read more."

Claire glanced at her. "What changed?"

Evelyn thought about it, surprised by the question and by how easily it came. "I got tired," she admitted.

Claire didn’t answer right away. She turned a page, then rested her hand there.

“Being tired is honest,” she said.

Evelyn sensed an understanding between them.

They stayed together while the treatments ran, the minutes passing without being counted. Outside the window, the dock kept its rhythm. Trucks arrived, doors opened, and crates moved from hand to hand. The work went on whether anyone looked at it or not.

Near the end of the infusion, Evelyn shifted in her chair. Her body felt like a sandbag slowly filling with wet sand, each grain settling deeply, intensifying the weight. The heaviness had grown denser, making every attempt to move like dragging the bag across rough ground. It wasn't pain, not yet. It was sheer weight, creeping in and anchoring her in place. She became aware of it the way you do when you've been holding something longer than you meant to. She looked at Claire, still reading, her attention steady, her posture unchanged, as if endurance were simply part of how she occupied space.

"I don’t know how much longer I can do this," Evelyn said. The words came out quieter than she expected.

Claire glanced up. She didn’t answer right away. She held Evelyn’s gaze without trying to soften it.

“It takes more out of me every time,” Evelyn went on. “I keep thinking I should be better at this by now. I should have learned how.”

Claire closed her book and rested it on her lap. “This isn't a skill that you learn,” she said. “Your body doesn't remember the last time. It only reacts to the present.”

There was no comfort in the sentence. No reassurance. Evelyn let it land anyway, solid and undeniable. She let it settle without arguing.

When the nurse came to disconnect their lines, they stood in unison and folded the quilt carefully, smoothing it before returning it to the basket. The fabric left her legs reluctantly. Evelyn felt its absence more than she expected.

Outside, the sun was bright. The dock was quieter now. The man in the reflective vest rested against the wall, drinking from a paper cup, his work paused for the first time that morning.

Evelyn walked to her car and sat behind the wheel without starting the engine. Her body ached in familiar places, but her mind felt clear. Something had moved, not enough to name, but enough to notice. She knew what she wanted to do next. She wasn't ready to say it yet. Not to anyone. Not even to herself.

She drove past her turn and continued toward the bluff road that curved along the south side of town. The houses there sat on large lots, set back from the street, cedar and fir trees breaking up the view. She pulled into a gravel turnout, shut off the engine, and looked across the water. The quiet arrived quickly. She took a deep breath to calm her mind, to escape the negative tunnel she had placed around herself.

When she finally returned home, the pain had settled further into her joints. She set her bag on the kitchen counter and left it there. The house held its silence easily. Her daughter lived across town now. Her husband lived near the docks. Their absence no longer bothered her, but tonight it felt wrong.

She stood at the sink and drank a glass of water, then another, waiting for the nausea to pass. It didn't.

She sat at the table until the daylight faded, then stood and made soup she couldn't finish. When she went to bed, sleep came and went without following a pattern. She woke before dawn with the familiar tightness in her upper chest and the dull pressure low in her abdomen. She lay still, breathing through it, waiting for her body to ease enough to let the day begin.

Later that week, the clinic called. Dr. Kwan wanted to see her.

The exam room was down the hall from the infusion suite and faced the other side of the building. There was no dock outside the window, no movement to follow. Just a narrow strip of sky and the tops of trees, their branches blurred by mist. Evelyn sat with her hands folded in her lap until Dr. Kwan came in, carrying a folder she recognized before he opened it.

He sat across from her and looked at her for a moment longer than usual.

"Do you have someone staying with you?" he asked.

"No," Evelyn said. "I've been on my own for the past five years."

He nodded and opened the folder.

He moved through the pages carefully, not rushing. The scans were laid side by side. The difference between them was small, but unmistakable. The cancer had gained ground. The treatment was no longer holding it in place. He spoke in measured language. Another round might slow things down for a while. There were adjustments they could try. New medications. Experimental options. None of them promised a reversal. He slid the papers across the desk toward her.

"Take these home," he said. "Read them when you're not tired. We can talk again whenever you're ready."

Evelyn looked down at the pages. Charts. Numbers. Words chosen to avoid hope and panic alike.

"How much longer?" she asked.

Dr. Kwan met her eyes. "That depends on what you choose to do."

She nodded. There was nothing more she needed from the conversation.

At home, she spread the papers across the table, read them once, then again. She followed the lines with her finger. Progression. Limited response. Increasing burden. The language was clear. She thought of the infusion room and the cold that crept into her the longer she sat still. The weight that stayed with her long after she left. Then she thought of Claire, reading beside her, steady in a way that felt chosen.

The next morning, she woke with the decision already in place. It did not arrive with relief or fear. It simply was. She made coffee and drank it slowly at the window, watching a woman walk her dog along the street below. The dog stopped often. The woman waited. Nothing hurried them.

When she called the clinic, she asked for Dr. Kwan.

"I don't want to continue treatment," she said.

He asked if she was certain. She said she was. He told her what support would look like now. Blood work. Pain management. Hospice. Regular check-ins. He told her she could change her mind at any point.

"I won't," she said.

She hung up and remained at the table for a long time afterward.

The following week, Evelyn returned to the hospital for blood work. She arrived later than usual and moved more slowly. She checked in, took the clipboard, and walked to the chairs near the window to wait for her turn to be called.

Claire was already there.

They noticed each other at the same moment. Claire's IV was in place. Her book lay open on her lap. She glanced at Evelyn's arm, bare.

"You're not hooked up," Claire said.

"No," Evelyn said.

Claire studied her face, not asking anything yet. "Are you all right?"

Evelyn considered the question. "I'm finished," she said.

Claire closed her book and rested her hands on it.

"With treatment," Evelyn added. "It isn't working."

Claire nodded once. She didn't argue. She didn't try to talk her out of it. "Do you want to talk about it?"

"Yes," Evelyn said. "But not here."

They shared the quilt anyway. It lay across their legs as it always had. The room felt colder than usual. When the nurse called Evelyn's name, Claire reached out and touched her wrist briefly. It was the first time either of them had done that.

Evelyn went for her blood draw and returned a few minutes later. Claire was still there. They sat together until Claire's infusion finished. When Claire stood, she hesitated.

"There's that coffee place on Main Street," she said. "If you feel up to it."

Evelyn nodded. "I do."

They walked out together, not rushing. A light mist lay low. The road flowed gently toward town. Below the hospital, the houses sat closer together, well-kept, with porches facing the street. On Main, the shops were open and busy, people walking their dogs. A man stood outside the coffee shop, holding the door open for someone inside. They took a corner table by the window overlooking the water. Evelyn wrapped her hands around the mug and let the heat sink in.

"I read the paperwork," she said. "It's not working anymore."

Claire listened without interrupting.

"I can't keep doing this," Evelyn continued. "Not the way it's taking everything from me. I know you're still going. I admire that. This dose isn't working, and I don't have anything else to give."

Claire shook her head. "It's not the same," she said. "The treatments don't ask the same things from any of us."

Evelyn felt the truth of that settle. She looked at Claire and felt the unexpected sting of gratitude.

"I'm glad I met you," she said.

Claire smiled, soft and unguarded. "I'm glad we met, too."

They sat talking until the coffee cooled, and neither felt the need to speak again. Outside, the street moved at its usual pace. Nothing marked the moment, but Evelyn knew her life had shifted.

She called her daughter two days later and said she wanted to talk. Rachel arrived with groceries she had not been asked to bring and set them on the counter without taking off her coat. She moved through the kitchen quickly, opening cabinets, rearranging things that did not need rearranging, speaking before Evelyn had finished a sentence.

When Evelyn told her, Rachel stopped moving. She stood with her back to the sink, hands braced on the edge, as if waiting for something else to be added. When nothing came, she shook her head once and began to argue. Not loudly. Not unkindly. She listed options, asked questions that assumed answers could still be changed, spoke of second opinions and new protocols she had read about online.

Evelyn let her speak. She watched the color rise in her daughter's face, the way fear tightened her voice.

"I'm not changing my mind," Evelyn said when Rachel paused to breathe.

Rachel stared at her. "You don't get to decide that alone."

"I already did," Evelyn replied.

Rachel's eyes filled, but she did not cry. She gathered her purse and went into the bathroom, closing the door with care. Evelyn heard the fan turn on. She sat at the table and waited.

That evening, Thomas called. He did not say how he had heard. He asked how she was feeling. He asked if she was certain. His voice stayed even, careful. When he finished asking what he needed to ask, he mentioned the loose step on the back porch and said he could fix it.

"You don't need to," Evelyn said.

"I know," he replied. "I'd still like to."

He came the next day with his own tools and worked without coming inside. She watched him from the kitchen window as he measured, tightened, and tested the step with his weight. When he finished, he stood on the porch for a while, looking out at the yard.

"Rachel's angry," he said when she stepped outside.

"She's scared," Evelyn answered.

He nodded. "So am I."

There was nothing more to say. He gathered his tools and left without touching her.

Claire came later that week with soup and stayed longer than either of them had planned. She sat on the couch, feet tucked beneath her, listening while Evelyn spoke. Not in any organized way. She talked about Rachel as a child, remembering when Rachel had a laugh that could fill the whole house, echo through the rooms, and make even the silent moments feel complete. There were stories about how a house fills up as someone grows and empties again when they leave. About being married to Thomas. About the arguments that had started small and accumulated until they no longer knew what they were arguing about.

"They felt so important at the time," Evelyn said. "Now I can't even remember what most of them were."

Claire didn't interrupt. She didn't try to sort it out. She stayed.

That night, after Claire left, Evelyn lay awake staring at the ceiling. The house settled around her. She thought of the infusion room, the shared quilt, the ease that had arrived without effort. She thought of how little it had taken to sit beside Claire and how much effort it now took to hold her ground with the people who loved her.

The thought came quietly. If she asked for another round of treatment, it would calm them. It would buy time. Not for her body, but for them, for their hearts. She pictured Rachel sleeping through the night. Thomas is repairing things without watching her so closely. Claire continuing her treatments without having to carry her added weight. The idea startled her. It did not come from fear of dying. It came from a love that she thought was gone.

The next morning, she called Claire and asked if she wanted to walk by the water.

They followed the path along the shore, the air cool and damp, gulls calling across the flats. They walked for a while without speaking, the rhythm of their steps steady.

"I almost asked for more treatment," Evelyn said.

Claire stopped. She turned and waited.

"Not because I want it," Evelyn went on. "Because I don't want them to hurt."

Claire looked out over the water, then back at her. "If you do it for that reason," she said, "you'll be carrying their pain along with your own."

Evelyn felt the truth of that settle in, heavy and unmistakable. She nodded and started walking again. Claire fell into step beside her.

They walked to the end of the path and turned back. They didn't need to say anything more. Evelyn knew the crisis had passed, not because the ache was gone, but because she had faced it and let it go without asking someone else to hold it for her.

After that, things began to change, not all at once, and not in ways that could be seen. Rachel stayed longer when she came and spoke less. Thomas began stopping by to sit on the porch, leaving before dinner without explanation. Claire finished a round of treatment and showed small signs of improvement, the kind that didn't invite celebration but could not be ignored. Evelyn's strength continued its steady decline.

The balance among them shifted without announcement. Days shortened. Light thinned. Each of them carried what they could and, without discussion, learned what to set down.

Claire started coming by in the mornings. Not every day, but often enough that Evelyn stopped wondering who was at the door when she heard the knock. She never came empty-handed, though she avoided the things people usually brought. No casseroles wrapped in foil. No bread that had dried out before it was served. She brought yogurt, washed fruit, and soup in small enough containers to finish. She moved through the kitchen carefully, asking where things were instead of assuming. She waited for answers.

They fell into a rhythm that didn't pretend to be temporary. Some days they talked easily, about small things: the way the fog lifted unevenly over the water, how the grocery store always had a faint scent of oranges, no matter the season. Other days, they sat together without speaking, the quiet stretching and easing between them without pressure. Evelyn realized she didn't brace herself around Claire. She didn't rehearse what she might say or soften what she meant. Words came when they came. Silence did too.

Her body continued to recede. Walks shortened, then slowed. She learned which chairs held her best and which windows tired her eyes. Pain arrived without warning now, sometimes sharp, sometimes dull, sometimes both at once. She adjusted when she could. She rested when she couldn't. She accepted help without comment.

Rachel returned often, her moods shifting. Some days she was brisk, almost cheerful. Other days, she moved through the house as if searching for a life she had misplaced. She cleaned the bathroom twice in one afternoon. She reorganized drawers no one had opened in years. Evelyn watched her and felt the pull of guilt rise and then loosen. She no longer tried to manage it.

Thomas came by less often, but when he did, he stayed. He stopped fixing things. Instead, he sat with her. They spoke about neighbors, about the weather turning. Once, without ceremony, he apologized. He didn't explain why. Evelyn accepted it without revisiting the past. The apology didn't change the space between them, but it gave them peace.

As the weeks passed, Claire's health began to take on a different shape. The nausea eased. The exhaustion no longer flattened her for days. One afternoon, sitting in the room filled with sunlight, Claire managed a soft laugh. "I think I'm finally winning the battle with my sofa," she joked, referring to the days when it had been her constant companion. Evelyn chuckled, the sound lightening the weight in the air. She spoke carefully of improvement, choosing her words as if they mattered, and Evelyn listened, feeling something warm and complicated rise in her chest. Relief, sorrow, and gratitude threaded through both of them.

"You'll ring the bell soon," Evelyn said one afternoon as they sat together on the couch. Claire nodded. "I think I might."

Evelyn's decline was gentler than she had expected, though no less real. There were hours when her mind stayed clear, when she followed conversations and noticed small things, and others when her thoughts drifted and returned without pattern. Claire learned to recognize the shifts. She lowered her voice. She slowed her movements. She waited longer before speaking again. Rachel learned too, though more unevenly. She asked fewer questions now. She stopped trying to plan past the day in front of them.

One evening, as the light thinned and the house settled into quiet, Evelyn felt a weight press in. No doubt about her choice, but something close to regret. She looked at Claire, sitting across from her with a book open but untouched, and allowed the thought to reach the surface.

"If I had met you earlier," Evelyn said, keeping her voice composed, "I might have kept going longer."

Claire looked up, surprised, and waited.

"Not because you would have talked me into it," Evelyn said. "Because being near you makes things feel possible."

Claire closed the book and set it aside. She took Evelyn's hand and held it.

"You didn't stop because you ran out of strength," she said. "You stopped because you knew what it was costing you."

Evelyn nodded. The words didn't comfort her, but they settled her mind.

A few days later, when the pain grew harder to manage, and sleep came only in fragments, Evelyn asked Claire to stay the night. Claire agreed without hesitation. She slept in the chair beside the bed, waking whenever Evelyn stirred, bringing water, adjusting pillows, staying close without turning it into a vigil.

In the early morning, Evelyn woke and found Claire watching her. She closed her eyes again, comforted by the feeling of another person, a friend, nearby.

As the days narrowed, the house filled quietly. Rachel slept on the couch. Thomas came and went, careful with his presence. Conversations softened and slowed. No one named what was coming.

On the last afternoon, Evelyn asked for the quilt. The nurse from the hospital brought it and said it was hers to keep. Claire unfolded it and laid it across Evelyn's legs, smoothing the edges as she had done that first day in the infusion room. Evelyn watched her hands and smiled.

"Stay," she said.

"I'm here," Claire replied.

Evelyn let herself rest, the weight of the quilt bringing her comfort and familiar memories.

The night passed in pieces. Sleep, waking, sleep again. The light outside shifted, gray pressing in, then thinning. Claire stayed in the chair beside the bed, her shoes set beneath it. She stood when needed. She sat when there was nothing to do. She learned the rhythm of Evelyn's breathing and followed it.

Rachel woke just after dawn and stood in the doorway for a long moment before coming in. She moved quietly, as if the sound of her footsteps might change things. She knelt next to the bed and took her mother's hand. Thomas arrived later, carrying nothing. He stood at the foot of the bed until Evelyn opened her eyes and looked at him.

"Come closer," she said.

He did, and sat where Claire had been sitting, his hands resting on his knees. She reached out and took his hand in hers.

Evelyn's voice was faint, but clear. "I'm sorry, too. It wasn't all your fault."

She asked Rachel to open the curtains a little. She asked Thomas for water. She thanked Claire for staying.

At one point, Rachel broke. She pressed her forehead to the mattress and cried, the sound sudden in the quiet room. Evelyn lifted her hand and rested it against her daughter's hair.

"You don't have to be strong now," she said.

Rachel stayed where she was.

Later, when the house had quieted again, Evelyn asked Claire to come closer.

"I don't regret it," Evelyn said. "I was afraid I might."

Claire met her gaze. "I know."

Evelyn looked toward the window. The soft rain had lifted enough to show the tops of trees and the slight line of the road beyond. Somewhere down the hill, a dog barked.

"I love each of you," Evelyn said.

"And we each love you," Claire answered.

Evelyn closed her eyes. Her breathing slowed, then changed. Rachel noticed first and tightened her grip. Thomas leaned forward. Claire stayed where she was.

When Evelyn died, it was without struggle. Her body eased into stillness. The room held that stillness for a long moment afterward.

They stayed. No one spoke. Claire folded the quilt and placed it at the foot of the bed.

Weeks later, Claire returned to the hospital, not for treatment, but to ring the bell.

The infusion room was unchanged. The chairs sat where they always had. The windows faced the dock, where a truck idled and a man lifted crates by hand. The bell hung near the nurses' station, polished and waiting. A few people gathered. Someone offered a tissue. Claire did not take it.

She rang the bell once. The sound carried, then faded. Applause followed, then quiet. Claire stood with her hand on the rope a moment longer. She rang it again, this time softly, for Evelyn.

Before she left, Claire walked to the basket near the wall. She unfolded the quilt and smoothed it, the way she always had, the way she had that first morning she met Evelyn, and again at the end. She laid it carefully on top of the others, not apart from them, not set aside. Someone else would be cold. Someone else would sit while the drugs did their work. The quilt would continue to do its job, bringing comfort and warmth to those who needed it.

Claire stepped into the cold fall air and felt what she carried settle into something she could live with. She knew now that survival was not the only measure. That staying mattered. That leaving, when done honestly, could teach the living how to remain.

She walked down the hill toward town, carrying Evelyn with her, not as grief, but as love.

On The Dock

The sound of the crunch of gravel announced the arrival long before the car came into view. It was a sound that lingered, much like the sharp scent of pine mixed with the cold bite of fall air from the lake. My wife and I stood on the porch, waiting. My daughter and her husband waved from the front seats, a quick flick of their hands. She called last night and said they were headed to a concert in the city. It was a last-minute thing, she explained, the tickets already bought. Our grandson didn't want to go, so she asked if he could stay the night.

The boy stepped out of the backseat with his backpack slung carelessly over one shoulder, his phone already in hand. Didn't even look at the house. The car door closed behind him, and the vehicle was reversing before he stepped away. They were gone that fast.

I stayed on the porch. My wife went down first, wrapping the boy in a hug like she'd been waiting all night for it. Maybe she had. The boy stood through it, polite enough. He gave a small smile when he saw me and headed up the steps.

Inside, our house held the kind of warmth that comes from age: the heat a little higher than necessary, the faint smell of stew still in the air. My wife had made extra, even though she'd said he probably wouldn't be hungry. She always cooked like someone might need comforting.

He stood near the doorway, not quite settled. He didn't take off his jacket. He was taller than last time, maybe thinner too. He kept checking his phone, texting his friends, maybe playing a game.

My wife asked if he wanted anything to eat. The boy shook his head without looking up.

The silence hung between us, a tangible presence filling the room. My wife glanced at me, the corners of her mouth tightening in a subtle question, one we both understood after all these years. The boy shifted in his seat, his shoulders rising slightly as he adjusted his phone. His fingers danced across the screen in a restless rhythm, his brow furrowing as if searching for a way to make the quiet vanish. We let the silence be.

I watched the boy from the kitchen table. I remembered back when he would run through this house barefoot, laughing like it was the funniest thing in the world. He'd skid across the floor, the soles of his feet blackened from play, shrieks of joy echoing down the hallway. In those days, his laughter was like the wind in the trees, unstoppable and wild.

Now he barely made a sound.

I reached for the newspaper out of habit, though I already knew what was in it. Across the room, the boy sat on the couch, bent over his screen, lit by a world that didn't include us.

I could hear the quiet sounds of my wife in the kitchen, rinsing something that didn't need rinsing, moving slowly on purpose. She always gave people time to settle. She never filled the silence unless it needed it.

The boy hadn't said much, hadn't needed to. At that age, his presence was the most you could ask for.

I thought about my daughter, how she'd once fit on my lap, all elbows and questions, too curious to ever sit still. Now she dropped off her own son, as if she were doing her parents a favor. Maybe she was. I didn't hold it against her. Sometimes life rushed people along faster than they meant to go.

I looked over at the boy again. Still folded into his phone, still somewhere else. But he was here, in our house. Breathing our air. And that felt good.

I sat back and let the room settle. Let the quiet be what it was. This was the shape our life had taken, slower, yes, but not less full. Just different.

And tonight, for one night, our grandson was with us.

We'd lived by the lake for twenty-two years, long enough that even the furniture seemed settled. I walked past the living room and glanced toward the mantel. Our wedding photo was still there, a picture from sixty years ago. We were full of optimism, making plans for a long life together. Back then, the idea of a quiet evening meant something entirely different.

The boy drifted through the room like it wasn't familiar anymore, like he was walking through a hotel. He dropped onto the couch, his thumbs tapping, a soft glow touching his face but not quite reaching his eyes. It was strange to see my grandson so physically present yet still seem so far away. But that was how it was now. I didn't take it personally.

My wife started dinner without a word, as she always did. The habit of setting plates, whether people were hungry or not, doesn't break easily. I sat at the table, listening to the soft rhythm of her moving in the kitchen, and under it, the sound of the boy's video, low enough to signal some awareness, if not engagement.

We ate together.

The boy answered our questions, not rudely, but with restraint. His fork moved his salad around, but he didn't pick anything up. He said school was fine, his dad was busy, and his mom was tired. He mentioned homework, though it didn't seem to be pressing. When his grandmother offered him pie, I said, "Maybe later," without looking up. At fourteen, he acted like there was a weight in him. That slight bend of the shoulders that comes when you already suspect the world won't make room for you.

After dinner, the boy retreated to the couch, folded into his phone's light. The room grew dim as evening fell, the gentle glow from the screen contrasting with the natural light fading through the windows.

I watched him from the doorway for a moment, then turned away. I remembered what it felt like to be that age, to think nothing truly important had happened before you were born. I didn't blame the boy. Life had to find you before you could understand it.

Later, my wife went to bed early. She always did now, not because she was tired of the day, but because she was tired in the way eighty years allows.

I stayed up after she went to bed, book in my lap, but my eyes weren't on the page. Across the room, the boy sat quietly, face lit by his screen, breathing shallow and even, that kind of stillness that only came from being completely absorbed elsewhere. I didn't mind. Just watched.

Outside, the lake had gone flat. Not a ripple in it. The porch light cast a pale square against the window, but it couldn't reach more than a few feet. Beyond that, nothing but dark.

I let my eyes rest there a while. Thought about the years, about how time had widened things. Not just distance you could measure, but the kind that creeps in, like fog rising from the lake at dawn. It shrouds the familiar, turning the landscape into something unrecognizable, much like the boy who sat across from me. The mist, much like the silence between us, made it feel normal not to talk. Until silence becomes the default. And still, even now, I believed in trying, even if the effort went unnoticed, hoping that one day the fog would lift, revealing what years had covered.

"Fishing tomorrow?" I asked.

The boy looked up, not startled. Just surprised to be spoken to. "Sure," he said, like someone agreeing to the weather.

I nodded. "We'll go early in the morning."

The boy went back to his phone.

Later, I moved down the hall without turning on the light. My wife was already asleep, steady breath, one hand resting above the quilt like always. I stood there a moment before getting in beside her. That familiar weight of her presence. Not heavy, just anchoring. I lay back and looked at the ceiling.

I thought about the boat. The still water. The way fishing had always been less about catching anything and more about sharing the space. I used to think that if someone stood beside you long enough, really stood there, they'd start to see what you saw.

Maybe tomorrow.

In the morning, the boy came into the kitchen wearing a hoodie and the same distant expression. He ate cereal standing up, phone propped against the sugar jar.

I poured coffee into the thermos the same way I always had. Slow, steady. The sandwiches were in a lunch basket. The boy didn't ask what kind.

We walked down to the dock, the stillness of the early morning surrounding us. The boards were damp from the night. I noticed that he stepped cautiously at first, testing the grip of his shoes, then eased up once he realized the wood wasn't slick.

I untied the boat with the same practiced motions I'd used for decades, stepped in with ease, and caught the boy's glance. Maybe he didn't expect me to move like that anymore.

The lake lay gray beneath a low sky, nothing dramatic, just the kind of morning stillness that kept sound close. Ripples spread evenly across the water as we pushed off. I started the engine, careful with the throttle, watching the boy, not to gauge interest, but to leave room. I didn't want to force anything. I wanted the day to shape itself.

Once we passed the no-wake marker, I gave a small nod.

"Ready to give it a try?" I asked, offering the wheel with a hint of invitation rather than obligation.

The boy's posture shifted immediately. The phone disappeared into a pocket without hesitation, and both hands took the wheel with an excited move. The hum of the engine came up through the deck, into the boy's arms, into his bones.

He leaned forward slightly, alert in a way he hadn't been before.

"Keep it steady," I said.

"I've got it," he replied, with the same determined look that he had years ago when I first let him take over the steering.

We crossed the lake toward one of my favorite spots. The boy kept his eyes fixed ahead, hands light but firm on the wheel. I watched him, not out of pride exactly, but out of something quieter. A kind of settled affection. This was what I wanted, not conversation, not proof. Just my grandson paying attention to the world.

We reached the spot, cut the engine, and let the boat drift. Cast out our lines. Waited.

Ten minutes in, the boy shifted. Reeled in. Checked the hook. Cast again.

He did the same thing five minutes later.

Then he checked his phone. Checked the time. Then the phone again. Occasionally, we could hear the echo of laughter carried over the water from a nearby home.

As I watched the boy, I talked about the bass that I had caught here a few weeks ago. I understood that stillness can feel uncomfortable to someone who's never had to sit in it.

Later in the morning, we motored over to the fuel dock. Not far. I let the boy take the wheel again. This time, no hesitation. His grip was firm, his back straight. He looked like he belonged there.

A familiar boat was tied up at the dock. A man stood at the pump, holding the nozzle in one hand and waving with the other, black, broad-shouldered, silver dusting his temples, with a wide smile.

When Edward saw us, his whole face lit up the way it always did: unguarded, genuine.

"Well, look at you," he called out. "Still out here acting like you own the lake."

I couldn't help but laugh, finding comfort in how natural it felt.

"Edward," I said, shaking my head. "Are you stealing fuel again?"

Edward stepped forward and held out his hand. We clasped palms and didn't let go right away. That small extra beat in the shake was something men did when they'd shared years, stories, and the weight of time.

Edward turned to the boy. "And who's this young man?"

"My teenage grandson," I said. "Here for the weekend."

"It can't be. Your grandson's a little boy. This young man is all grown up."

"That's what time does," the grandfather said.

That was good enough for Edward. He nodded, like everything that needed to be said was right there. “And he’s letting you drive the boat?”

The boy looked between them, hesitated, then said, “Yeah.”

Edward grinned. “He must really trust you. He won’t even let me get in his boat.”

We talked some more, then I paid, and untied the boat. Edward waved once more, already back in his own boat. As I drove off, I watched the boy keep his eyes on Edward.

As we slowed down to ease into another small cove, the boy said, “That guy’s probably too dumb to do anything but fish and eat watermelon.”

I didn’t turn. I didn’t say anything. I kept my hand steady on the throttle, eyes forward, the wake opening behind us. Within that silence, I couldn't help but think about where he might have picked up those words. Was it the constant chatter online, the subtle undercurrent of prejudice buried in social media, or perhaps a careless remark from a friend trying to shrug off seriousness with a joke? These were not just words flippantly spoken, but echoes of larger currents, seeded by a world that refuses to let go of old habits.

“His name is Edward Tillison," I said finally. "He lives three houses down from us. He's a close friend. Fixed this engine last summer when it wouldn’t start, brings over tomatoes every August, whether we ask for them or not."

“So?” the boy replied, face closed off.

I paused.

"What makes you say that about him?" I asked. My voice didn’t rise. “You just talked about someone you don’t know.”

No reaction.

I let the silence stretch, then added, “What if you’re wrong?”

Still nothing.

I didn't turn. If I did, my anger would show, and anger wasn't the point. Not here. Not now.

The boy finally muttered, "Whatever. You know what I mean."

I wanted to ask, "Do I?" I wanted to stop the boat, turn to the boy, and tell him exactly why words like that hollow people out.

But I didn't.

Because I knew what would happen, it would either make him retreat or double down. Neither would help.

I let the boat idle, the sound of the motor low beneath us.

"Where did you hear that?" I asked instead.

The boy shrugged. "I don't know. People say stuff. It's a joke."

"It wasn't funny," I said.

The boy looked at me now. "You're being sensitive."

The word struck me hard, not for what it meant, but for how casually it came, like a lid snapping shut.

I kept steady. "Edward is my friend."

The boy's mouth twitched. "So what, you have one Black friend, and now you're the race police?"

My grip on the wheel tightened before I noticed it. I made a point to loosen it, finger by finger. I didn't want my hands to say more than my mouth would.

"You met him," I said. "You saw how we talked. You think he got where he is by being dumb?"

The boy didn't answer. Just turned to the side and muttered, "You're making it a big deal."

And maybe I was. But not for the reason the boy thought. It wasn't the insult. It was the ease of it. How quickly something so small could reveal what had taken root. The boy had no idea what had come out of his mouth. No idea that some words stay.

I killed the motor. The boat drifted for a breath, then stopped with a tug as the anchor settled.

“It matters what you say about people,” I said. “It shapes how you treat them.” I nodded at the anchor line holding us steady in the water. “Like that rope. Our words have weight. They hold in ways you don’t always see.”

The boy exhaled, not quite a laugh. "Grandpa, it's not like I'm hurting anyone."

I let the silence stretch, absorbing what he'd said.

Then, "You hurt me. Edward was my sergeant in Vietnam."

My voice softened as I allowed the memory to surface, the vivid recall of that day heavy in the air. The smell of cordite clung to my memory, sharp and bitter, mingling with the metallic tang of blood.

"Edward saved my life," I added, my voice steady but low, letting the words paint the scene.

I didn’t look at the boy as I spoke. Just reached down, lifted the side of my shirt, and showed the jagged scar that ran along my ribs. Raw and ugly. Skin healed, but not smooth. The boy stared at it, mouth open.

“We were pinned down. A mortar hit close. Three men died. I wasn’t supposed to make it.”

I let the shirt fall.

“I don’t tell this story to anyone, even your mother. And I won’t again. But that man you just called dumb carried me back to the base on his shoulders. He saved my life.”

I let the weight of that settle. Let it take its shape between us.

“If not for him, your mother wouldn’t exist. Neither would you.”

The boy didn’t respond. His gaze moved from me to the water. The boat creaked gently. The wind shifted.

And then, soft enough that it barely reached me, the boy said, “I’m sorry, grandpa. I didn’t know.”

We stayed on the lake a while longer. Neither of us expected to catch anything. That wasn’t the point anymore. The boy reeled in and adjusted his hook with more care than before. Cast again.

I watched him do it. Didn’t say a word.

Eventually, the boy set the rod down across his knees and reached for his phone. He didn’t turn it on. Just held it a while, turning it over in his hands, before tucking it back into his pocket.

We ate the sandwiches slowly. The bread had gone soft in the cooler. The boy wiped his hands on his jeans without thinking. Somewhere, far off, a fish jumped and disappeared again.

Later, the boy said, “We should head back.” Not stiff. Not defensive. Just honest.

I nodded. Turned the key. The motor hummed to life. The shoreline drew closer, slow and solid. Trees. Docks. The boy didn’t speak.

At the dock, I climbed out, and he tied the rope the way he'd been shown years ago. He checked it himself, twice, glanced at me, nodded once, and followed me up the path without a word.

We walked back to the house side by side. Nothing remarkable in the way our feet moved. One foot hit the path, the other followed, and for a moment it felt like the space between us wasn’t quite so wide. Not gone, not fixed, but smaller.

Inside, the familiar quiet of the house settled around us. The boy went straight to the couch and picked up his phone. The screen lit his face, the old habit settling back in easily, like an old coat worn too many times. He brushed invisible crumbs off his jeans, fingers moving absently, a sign of his restlessness.

I lingered in the doorway a moment, watching, then turned toward the kitchen, already thinking about what we might eat. Simple things. Nothing fancy.

Midafternoon came, and with it my daughter and her husband. They arrived full of quick smiles, quick questions, and thanks offered. His mother hugged the boy first, then hugged us with the kind of urgency people carry when they're glad to be on schedule again. His father opened the backseat door for the boy and called a tired thank-you over his shoulder.

He hugged his grandmother, then me, a little tighter than before. There was something in his hold that wasn't quite the same. Not awkward. Not distant. Then the words, "I love you, grandpa."

He climbed into the car and closed the door. As the engine started, He waved once through the window. Then returned to his phone before the car had even backed out of the driveway.

We stood on the porch until the sound of the engine faded around the bend and then became nothing at all. I felt my wife's presence. Warm. Solid. Familiar.

She looked at me and saw a tear. She gave me time. After a moment, she asked, "How was it?"

I turned my head just enough to look at her, still as beautiful as she was sixty years ago.

"We saw Edward at the dock."

Her face softened gently, like sunlight through a curtain.

"Did I say how big your grandson has grown?" she asked.

"Yes," I said. "It's been a couple of years."

She didn't rush me. She just waited. Her patience wasn't passive. It was respect, the kind that comes from long experience.

Finally, I said, "The boy said a thing."

Her eyes narrowed slightly. "What kind of thing?" she asked.

I heard the boy's words again, unfiltered, raw, their sting still sharp even after the day had softened around us. I spoke them aloud, the way I felt them in my chest, letting them sit between us. Neither softened nor exaggerated, just there, clear and unembellished.

His wife's mouth tightened, small and subtle, the way someone narrows their gaze when they don't yet know where to rest it. She looked out toward the lake, not because the water was particularly interesting, but because she needed a place to put her eyes while she thought.

Our grandson, the baby we held at the hospital, the child who spent summers with us. The memories flashed by.

I said, "I corrected him."

"What did he do?" she asked, quiet, steady.

I let out a slow breath. "He apologized. Maybe it meant something, maybe it didn't."

She nodded once. Slow. Considered. "Maybe it did," she said. "He has a hard time showing his feelings."

I didn't tell her what came up inside me, not the texture of what I said, not the way the memory of Edward's sacrifice still lived in my chest. She already knew that Edward had saved my life. But the rest of it, the rest I kept in the place where it belonged: inside my own world, silenced forever.

She didn't ask for more. She didn't need details to understand the cost. After sixty years together, she could read my restraint as clearly as if I'd spoken whole paragraphs aloud.

We went inside. The familiar quiet of the house settled around us again. The afternoon passed wordlessly. We made dinner, though we weren't hungry. We cleaned up. Outside the windows, the sky darkened slowly, and the lake took on that metallic gray hue evenings always brought.

Later, we took our tea to the porch and sat down. The chairs were old and familiar, molded by years of evenings just like this, two bodies resting into habit.

"It's like each generation can't learn from the past. The war, civil rights, Kent State, it all has to be repeated," I said. "To hear my own grandson say words like that makes me wonder if I was ever that blind at fourteen."

I thought back to stories my father used to tell. He spoke of the Great Depression, not to evoke sympathy, but to share lessons learned in hard times. Shelves were empty, jobs lost, and adults struggled to hide their fear. His voice remained steady, as if by giving words to these trials, they might not repeat. I remember listening with half an ear, convinced his world was a relic of the past.

My wife recalled her grandfather's experiences in the war, tales of battles fought and conditions endured, details from places we'd never heard of. As a teen, she too only nodded in feigned understanding, eager to believe those struggles belonged to another time.

We both had believed, in the arrogance of youth, that those stories were far behind us. But time has a way of blurring such certainties.

"Those memories were very real to them, but they didn't mean anything to us."

"And now?" she asked.

My gaze drifted over the lake. A single light across the water came on, a small, steady point. "Now I know they were trying to pass something on," I said.

She sipped her tea without flinching, without a hint of forced optimism. She didn't say the boy would grow up and understand. Maybe he would. Maybe he wouldn't. She had stopped turning hope into certainty long ago.

After a while, she said, "We didn't listen either."

I turned my head slightly to look at her. Her expression was calm, not excusing or condemning, just naming a truth that kept bitterness at bay.

I felt the sting of it. Not quite shame, more like a shift in the way I saw the years behind me. A boy hears a story and shrugs. A man hears it years later and wonders how he ever thought he was separate from it.

"I wanted him to see Edward."

She didn't rush to comfort me. Didn't sweeten it with reassurance. She just said, "He saw him. He didn't know what he was seeing."

We sat in silence for a long moment. The lake drew in the last light of day. The air cooled around us, gentle and slow. Her hand rested on the arm of her chair, fingers relaxed. And as I watched those fingers, I remembered holding them once, in a hospital room years ago, when our daughter was born. I remembered holding them again in another room when her mother died. I remembered all the ordinary days in between, the ones no one wrote down.

Sadness came again, not as weight, but as shape. Less about the boy now and more about time itself: youth and adulthood and the strange territory of becoming old and looking back when the time to look forward was nearing an end.

Out on the lake, a fish broke the surface with a quick, sharp splash. Somewhere a loon called, distant, brief.

"I should have spoken more."

She looked at me with that quiet, steady regard that never needed eloquence.

"You spoke enough," she said. "You didn't turn it into a fight. You gave him a fact. Facts stay."

I knew she meant to give me something solid to hold onto. I accepted it.

We stayed on the porch a while longer, tea cooling in our cups, the lake now fully dark. The porch light made a small circle around us. Beyond it, night held its distance.

I thought of Edward again, his easy laugh, the steady hands that knew engines and nets and kindness, and how two men could become like brothers without much explanation.

I thought of my grandson's face when I corrected him, that moment when he apologized, and wondered if that conversation might ever come back to him with meaning.

My wife reached over and put her hand on my forearm. Not gripping and not pleading. Just making contact, our love summed up in a simple gesture.

I looked at her and felt the quiet truth of what was left between us. We had grown old together. We knew the world didn't get better in a straight line. We had learned to love what was near, to do what we could, to speak when it mattered, and to sit in silence without thinking it meant surrender.

She said, "Tomorrow we'll call Edward and check in."

We stayed on the porch until the air cooled, then they went inside, turned off the lights one by one, and carried the day to bed.

I Had A Horse Once

Luke arrived at the hospital just after six, the same time as the night before, and the night before that. The lemon-cleaner smell hung in the air, but just beneath it lay the scent of medicine, a reminder of where he was. The lights remained constant, bathing everything in an unchanging glow. The halls never got darker, just quieter.

Harold lay in the bed by the window. His mouth stayed open now. The way it had been since Tuesday. A tube ran under his nose, though Luke wasn't sure it still mattered. The last time Harold responded to anything was Sunday, when Luke had mentioned a bay gelding that kicked the trailer door off its hinges. Harold's lip had moved. Just barely.

Luke had seen death before. Not this kind, though, not the slow kind that takes days, pulling a man apart in inches, starting with his voice and ending with his shape. He looked smaller every evening. Not by much. Just enough that it couldn't be unseen.

He sat beside Harold now, in the same chair, in the same place. He didn't say hello. Just leaned in a little and started talking like he had the night before.

"They've moved the cattle off the back range," Luke said. "I saw the trailers pulling out yesterday morning. Dust everywhere. One of those red-faced drivers, you know the type, he nearly backed into the damn gate."

No answer, of course.

He let the silence sit there, let it grow a little. Then he kept going.

"I don't know if you remember that Appaloosa we bought out in Graham. The one with the crooked blaze. You said it looked like someone tried to paint it with their eyes closed. I rode past a place this morning that had one just like it. Same stance, too. Looked like it didn't trust the ground it stood on."

Harold's hand lay across his chest. Not curled, not open. Just there.

Luke remembered the last time they'd argued. Not a fight. Just one of those long, quiet disagreements about tack or teeth, floating, or whether you could break a filly without ever raising your voice. Harold had said you could. Luke hadn't believed him. He did now.

Outside the window, a car passed. Then another. Someone dropped a tray in the hallway. Luke didn't look.

He'd known Harold for fifteen years. Not friends at first; more like two men whose paths kept crossing. They found themselves hauling feed, checking hooves, and arguing over stall placement. Yet, one day, Harold brought an extra coffee in a paper cup and silently placed it in front of Luke. That quiet gesture marked the start of their friendship.

Luke looked at him now, his throat tightening with a silent constriction, a sensation that rose and fell, refusing to dissolve into tears. He averted his eyes slightly, unwilling to meet Harold's face directly, as if doing so might unravel the measured calm he was holding onto. This wasn't the kind of grief that demanded to be seen; it lingered quietly, waiting for its moment without making a sound.

From the other bed, the voice came out of nowhere. Low. Unclear.

"I had a horse once."

Luke turned, not fast. The voice was low, coming from the second bed. He hadn't expected it. The man hadn't spoken once in all the evenings Luke had been there. Just lay there, angled toward the curtain, half-swallowed by the bed, eyes open sometimes, sometimes not.

Luke didn't say anything at first. He glanced back at Harold, whose breathing was thin but steady. Then back toward the man on the other side of the room. The voice hadn't sounded strained. Just distant.

Luke took a small step toward the curtain, but didn't speak. He didn't want to crowd him.

The door opened. A nurse came in with a clipboard in one hand and a slight frown on her face, the kind that came from habit, not concern. She moved toward Harold's side of the room but stopped mid-step, looking across the curtain.

"I had a horse once," the man said again, though quieter now.

"Mr. James?" she said, like she couldn't trust what she'd heard.

He didn't move. Just stared at the same spot on the wall, as if the words had left him but hadn't asked permission to do it.

She looked at Luke, lowering her voice.

"That's the first thing he's said since admission," she whispered. "Four days now. Nothing. Not a word."

Luke nodded, uncertain what to do with that. The man's presence had always felt like background. A shape in the bed. He hadn't thought to ask for more.

Luke cleared his throat lightly. "What kind of horse?"

The old man didn't answer right away. Then, "Don't matter."

The nurse moved in closer, near Luke's ear. "Would you please?" she whispered. "He won't talk to us."

Luke looked at her, then back at the man. Something about the way he'd spoken, those five words, held a thread. It wasn't an invitation exactly. But it wasn't to be ignored. Perhaps there was more to unravel. Luke leaned slightly forward. "Tell me more about your horse," he asked softly, letting the question hang as he allowed the silence to invite whatever Mr. James needed to share. He moved his chair carefully to make the motion feel easy. Not a shift in attention, just a man taking a seat. He stayed half-turned toward Harold's bed, keeping that connection.

The man didn't turn his head, but his voice came clearer now, shaped by something slower than thought, a distant memory trying to take shape in words.

"I was fifteen when my Daddy brought him home," he said.

Luke leaned back in his seat, like he was giving the words a place to settle.

"We lived on a farm in Mississippi, near Greenwood. Raised cotton. Not a big place, not good land either, but Daddy worked it. My two older brothers helped some. Not much once they got their diplomas. They took off the same year. One headed north, the other got married and moved to Yazoo."

The man's voice was weak, but it had direction.

"My mama died when I was ten. After that, it was just the four of us. Then the two. Just him and me. I was still in school. Did what I could before and after class, but I knew it was too much for him. He didn't say anything, but you could see it in how slow he moved by sundown."

Luke watched the side of the man's face, the way his jaw tensed every few lines, like the telling was painful, but necessary.

"We held on for two more years, then he sold it. Said the land had already taken more than it gave. Bought a place south of Dallas. Had a barn, about twenty acres. Couldn't grow anything. But we didn't need to. That's what he said. Didn't need to."

The man's breath caught slightly. Not emotion. Just age.

"That's when he brought Ned home."

Luke asked, "That was the horse's name?"

"Yep."

Nothing more for a long moment.

"Less than a year old. Colt stepped off the trailer with his legs spread like he didn't know which way to run. Didn't take more than a glance to see he was scared of his own breath."

The man's hand shifted under the blanket, barely noticeable.

"My Daddy didn't say why he got him. Just handed me the lead rope, said, 'You take good care of him, son, and he'll be the best friend you ever had.' Then he walked back inside. It was like he'd just handed me a shovel or a hammer. Guess he knew that if I cared, I'd learn."

That line settled in Luke's chest. It didn't need explaining. It had weight by itself.

"I didn't know what I was doing. Never been near a horse longer than five minutes. Read every book I could find. Asked questions when people had time to answer. But most of what I learned came from Ned. And most of what he gave, he gave slowly."

The room had stilled. Even Harold's machines, for a moment, seemed quieter.

"He'd freeze if I moved too fast. Wouldn't eat if I stood too close. So I stopped trying to make him do anything. I just showed up. Every morning, every night. Sat in the stall sometimes without saying a word. He started coming closer."

Luke remembered that kind of learning, when the lesson wasn't about technique but about presence.

"Took a full year before he'd follow me without a rope. Another six months before he let me put a saddle blanket on him. I thought the first ride would be something big, that he'd be bucking, maybe kicking. But he just stood there. Like he'd already decided he was mine."

The man paused. No need to hurry. He was telling the memory.

Luke stayed still, letting him hold that memory without crowding it.

"Ned started learning tricks early. I didn't push him into anything. Just tried things, and he picked them up fast. Seemed to like it. Playing around. Learning something. Being seen."

He closed his eyes for a moment, then opened them again.

"By the time I graduated, we were tight. I mean tight. Never rode him, though. Not once. Hadn't even put a saddle on him yet."

He shifted again in the bed. Luke noticed how slow the movement had gotten.

"My Daddy died a week after I finished high school. Sat down in his chair and never got back up. Stroke, they said. My brothers came back, thought they were gonna split things. Found out that the house and most of the money were left to me. They took their checks, didn't stay long."

He paused, let that memory settle on its own.

"I stayed. Started selling insurance with a friend. Nothing big. But it kept the lights on, fed both Ned and me."

Luke watched his hands, resting now, still. No shake. Just settled.

"I decided to train him myself. Didn't want anybody else putting their hands on him. Read more. Talked to folks. Then one day, I brought home a saddle and pad. Put 'em on the fence. Took him over slow."

He breathed in again, and this time it caught a little.

"He just stood there. Didn't blink. I went really slow. Put the pad on first. No reaction. Then the saddle. Still nothing. So I got on."

Luke raised his eyebrows slightly. That part had come fast.

"Figured he'd jump, maybe sidestep. He didn't even flick his ears. Just looked ahead. Bored, almost. So I rode him. That was it."

The old man went quiet again.

Luke didn't fill the space. He wanted it to last.

"We didn't stay local much after that," Mr. James said. "I started loading him in the trailer on weekends. Then longer trips. Pretty soon, we were covering half the country."

His voice had picked up a thread of energy now, not bright exactly, but steadier.

"We'd drive out to the Rockies. Utah. Arkansas hills. Anywhere with trails and quiet. I'd find places to camp, let him graze while I built a fire. He never wandered. Just stayed near, like he figured out that the world only worked right if we were close."

Luke felt that line land in his chest. There was something in it, not just companionship, but the way a life reorganized itself around another being. He didn't look at Harold. He didn't need to. That feeling was already stretching across both beds.

"He learned some tricks," Mr. James said. "Not because I taught him how, but because we spent so much damn time together. He'd steal my hat, wait till I bent down to pick it up, then bump me from behind. Always waited till I was bent over to make sure I would stumble. Folks thought that was hilarious."

Luke smiled without meaning to. Not wide. Just enough that it reached behind his eyes.

"He'd play tag with me. I'd chase him around the pasture, then turn, and he'd follow me like a damn dog. People used to come by to watch us."

The rhythm slowed.

"But he never did it for them. He only did it when I asked. Only when it was me."

The quiet returned, and this time it held.

Luke thought about the way some men told stories — not to relive them, but to let them out before they faded. And how few people ever heard the ones that mattered.

Mr. James hadn't moved much since he started talking, but Luke noticed now how still his hands had become. One rested near the edge of the blanket, just visible. Open. Not clenched.

"I was forty when I met my wife," Mr. James said.

He didn't change position when he said it. Didn't brace for reaction. Just stated it, like a marker you drive into the ground so you know where you are.

"We'd been on the road a long time by then. I wasn't looking for anybody. She was visiting someone nearby and came out to the place one afternoon. Asked about the horse."

Luke noticed how his mouth tightened slightly on that last word.

"She liked the idea of Ned. Liked watching him move. But she didn't like the quiet. Didn't like how far everything was from town. We got married anyway."

A pause. Short. Functional.

"For a while, it worked. Or maybe I just told myself it did."

Luke shifted his weight slowly. He'd heard this part before in other voices, other rooms, the moment when attention thins, not because of cruelty, but because life demands it somewhere else.

"I didn't stop taking care of Ned," Mr. James said. "Just didn't spend as much time with him. Thought he wouldn't notice. Horses notice."

That landed. Luke didn't look at Harold. He stayed with the voice.

"One afternoon, I found him out in the pasture, lying flat. Legs wrong. Breathing shallow. Thought he was dead."

The words came out faster now. Not rushed. Just closer together.

"I ran to him. Lost one boot in the mud. Couldn't get my hands to work right. Vet came out, gave him shots. Told me to keep him still. I slept in the barn that night. Sat there listening to him breathe."

Luke felt his jaw tighten. That image stayed. A man sitting awake beside something that might leave before morning.

"He was better the next day," Mr. James said. "Stood up slowly. Walked over and bumped me with his head. Like he was reminding me that he was still there."

Silence.

"That fixed it for me," he went on. "I started spending time with him again. Not like before. But enough."

"She wanted to move into town," Mr. James said. "I said no. Didn't argue. Just no. She left after that. Didn't make much of a mess. Took what she wanted. That was the end."

Luke watched his face. No anger surfaced. No relief either. Just the shape of a decision that had already finished doing its work.

"He got older after that," Mr. James said. "Slowed down. His back end started hurting. The vet said it was arthritis. Medicine didn't do much."

Luke thought of Harold again then, the way his hands no longer closed all the way, the way time narrowed the body to small movements without asking permission.

"I put air conditioning in part of the barn," Mr. James said. "People thought I was crazy. But the heat was getting to him. He'd stand in there during the day, chewing hay like he'd found himself a palace. At night, I'd let him out. He liked the pond. Would stand in it up to his knees."

Luke could see it. Clear as anything.

"He didn't meet me at the gate every night anymore. But sometimes he did. Would whinny when I drove up, turn around a couple times. Not for food. Just to let me know he saw me."

The room held still around that.

"I came home one afternoon and found him there," Mr. James said. "By the gate. Lying down like he'd just decided he was done."

Luke felt that line settle deep, heavy.

"I buried him right there," Mr. James went on. "Took me all night and most of the next day. Dug it myself."

Luke could picture it. The ground hard, maybe root-knotted. Maybe clay. The digging that quiets your body with pain but gives you something to do with grief. He tried to imagine it clearly, a man alone, a light somewhere nearby, the sound of metal in dirt.

"Except for those first few months, Ned was with me every day for thirty-two years. My Daddy was right. He was my best friend. We took care of one another."

The room had gone still. Even the noise from the hallway, the occasional call light, the low wheel roll of a cart, seemed to pull back. Luke could hear Mr. James's voice thinning.

"He died forty-five years ago, and not a day passes that I don't think about him. Forty-five years. Now I'm hoping that what they say about horses being in Heaven is true. I'm hoping to see him again. Forty-five years is a long time to be away from your best friend."

Mr. James closed his eyes.

There was no collapse, no dramatic final note. Just a closing, soft and unannounced, like someone stepping into another room and letting the door rest gently behind them.

Luke watched his frail body as his breathing slowed.

The rise and fall of the chest took on a wider distance. The kind of pause between breaths that told you something in the rhythm had changed.

A couple of nurses came into the room, listening now. One by the door. One a little closer. Neither moved, not yet. No clipboard. No adjustment. Just presence.

The tears did not fall.

They stayed where they were, caught, as if even that small release required more strength than they had left.

Luke stayed in the chair. His hands rested on his knees, fingers lightly touching. Not folded and not clenched.

He listened to Mr. James's breathing as it slowed and deepened. His lips moved ever so slightly.

Luke didn't look for meaning in it. He just stayed inside it, where it was quiet, where nothing needed fixing.

Harold did not move.

His face remained slack, his mouth slightly open. Luke knew not to mistake stillness for absence. But this stillness felt different. Not because it was final, but because it asked nothing more of anyone.

Mr. James lay with his eyes closed. His breathing had changed again. It was no longer paced. No longer part of the room's rhythm. It had separated itself, like a clock that had decided time wasn't necessary anymore.

A nurse stepped closer.

She didn't announce anything. Didn't speak. Just reached across and checked the monitor. The line was still moving, but slower. Uneven.

She stood back, waiting, her hand now resting lightly against the edge of the bed.

Luke looked from one bed to the other. Two men at the end of their lives. One speaking, one silent. Both held by memories that had done their work and could do no more.

He thought of how little of a life could be carried forward and how much of it remained sealed inside the person who lived it. Things never said. Things never written down. Things no one else would know unless they happened to be sitting in a chair at the right time, on the right night.

Mr. James shifted once, his face tightening briefly, then easing.

"Ned," he said, as he let out a breath.

The nurse reached out and touched Luke's arm. Not urgently. Just enough.

A small signal that the moment had arrived.

Luke stood and moved back.

He didn't rush. He didn't speak. He gave the room its quiet back.

He paused at the curtain and looked once more at the two beds.

Harold lay as he had all week, receiving words he could not answer. His presence was steady, unresponsive. And still somehow... there.

Mr. James lay still now, his story finished.

Luke stepped into the hallway.

Behind him, the door clicked shut. It wasn't loud, but it felt like something final. The corridor was nearly empty now, and most of the lights dimmed. It must've been close to midnight.

He stood there for a moment. His body felt slower than it should have. Not heavy, just used. The way you feel after sitting too long with something that mattered.

No one passed. No questions. The nurses' station down the hall had gone quiet. A monitor beeped faintly from another room, but it didn't seem urgent. Nothing moved.

He walked to the elevators and pressed the button. The hallway floor gave under his feet with that soft linoleum bounce, the kind hospitals always had.

When the doors opened, he stepped inside. No hesitation. No drama.

The ride down was silent. There was nothing to say, not even to himself.

He walked out through the main lobby. A woman was mopping near the vending machines. She didn't look up.

The glass doors slid open without a sound. Outside, the air was cooler than he expected. The kind that settles over a town late at night when most people are already asleep. The sky didn't offer anything, no moon, no stars, just the reflection of streetlights in the parking lot.

He crossed to his truck.

There were only a few cars left now. One delivery van. A maintenance truck with a light bar. Everything else was still.

Luke opened the door, slid behind the wheel, and sat for a while before turning the key. He didn't rush. Didn't lean his head back. Just sat and thought about Mr. James and a horse named Ned.

He'd drive home in a bit, walk in, hold his wife tightly, and tell her how very much he loved her. He'd hug his dog, too, a golden retriever that he rescued from a junk yard years ago. But for right now, he wanted to shed a tear, not for sorrow, because dying is part of life, and not for happiness, because Mr James is back with Ned. His heart felt love, and in that feeling, there didn't need to be an explanation. In that silence, the tears came.

www.ingramcontent.com/pod-product-compliance
Lightning Source LLC
LaVergne TN
LVHW090538110826
845146LV00003B/1159